# How to Overcome

## Stormy Weather

### by Wayne W. Sanders

And when he was entered into a ship, his disciples
followed him. And, behold, there arose a great tempest in
the sea, insomuch that the ship was covered with
the waves: but he was asleep.

Matt 8:23-24 KJV

# How to Overcome

# Stormy Weather

by Wayne W. Sanders

BOLD TRUTH
PUBLISHING

Christian Literature and Artwork

A BOLD TRUTH Publication

ISBN 13: 978-0-9972586-0-8

Common Ground Ministries
P.O. Box 2811
Broken Arrow, Oklahoma 74013
www.cgmok.com
*waycon3@gmail.com*

BOLD TRUTH PUBLISHING
300 West 41st Street
Sand Springs, Oklahoma 74063
www.BoldTruthPublishing.com

# *Dedication*

I dedicate this book first of all to the one who inspired me the most to write it, Jesus Christ my Lord and Savior. To write down my thoughts on paper has proven to be quite the challenge for me. But through the many prayers and the support of my wife this book is now complete and ready to transfer to you the reader.

I would like to give a special thanks to a very close friend to our family, Miss. Gale Sherrill who spent countless hours proofreading and typing this manuscript while editing this book for me. Though it may not be a large book it has certainly been a challenge for her to capture my thoughts and bring clarity to them.

A simple thank you is not enough to express my gratitude for all my friends who saw me through to its completion as you supported, read and re-read this manuscript. And then guided me with your talents in designing the cover to the message and its content.

I would also like to thank Aaron Jones for enabling me to publish this book.

Last but not least: In all humbleness I sincerely ask that you find forgiveness for me in not naming the countless other friends that have stayed the course with me over all these years.

# Contents

# Contents

## *Introduction*

There are those times in everyone's life when it seems like you have been fenced in on every side and there is no way out. I remember a time when I was standing along the seashore while a big storm was brewing. The silence would be broken as every wave would come crashing down, one upon the other. I knew better than to get into the water. Yet, I would find myself wading in just to try and catch a ride on one of those magnificent waves. There is an excitement in the air as you face these kinds of challenges. You can call me stupid, if you want to, but I'm a thrill-seeker and always have been!

Then, there are those storms in life that suddenly come upon you when you are not expecting them. You are not necessarily fully prepared, if at all, to face them, and the waves come crashing down on you relentlessly. They have a tempo that seems to increase with each approaching wave. You can only get your head above water long enough to catch your breath. As you gasp for breath all sight of the safety of the shoreline seems to have been removed. There is a hopelessness that sweeps over you just at the thought of drowning.

1

*Psalm 89:9 NKJV*
*You rule the raging of the sea;*
*When its waves rise, You still them.*

It is in times like these that we need to raise up our voices to God, calling on Him in the Name of Jesus, and give Him the glory and the honor due Him. Set your gaze upon the Lord, for that is the way of escape. Focus on His great power and His abilities to deliver you out of all of your distresses. Life's circumstances may have you overwhelmed to the point that you cannot see your way out of your situation. The thunderous sounds of the waves have eroded your hope. God's voice is mightier than that thunderous sound and can drown out the devilish sounds of defeat. God calms the raging seas!

In this book, I would like to share with you things that have given me hope in the hopeless situations.

The Word of God is alive and can bring an answer to the everyday storms of life that try to attach to you. God can defeat the devil in your life, even if there is a messenger of Satan wanting to sift you.

*Luke 22:31-32 NIV*
*31 Simon, Simon, Satan has asked to sift you as wheat.*
*32 But I have prayed for you, Simon, that your faith may not fail. And when you have turned back, strengthen your brothers.*

Jesus said, *"But I have prayed for you."* Who has prayed for you? Jesus! That brings me great comfort. People sometimes say they are praying for me, and be that as it may, when Jesus says it, you can take it to the bank!

The stormy weather may make the edge of the sea seem to be an elusive and indefinable boundary. This is an attempt to deceive you and keep you away from the Master of the wind. God lives in the praises of His people, and with Him you can overcome any storm.

> *Psalm 93:3-5 NIV*
> *3 The seas have lifted up, O LORD,*
> *the seas have lifted up their voice;*
> *the seas have lifted up their pounding waves.*
> *4 Mightier than the thunder of the great waters,*
> *mightier than the breakers of the sea—*
> *the LORD on high is mighty.*
> *5 Your statutes stand firm;*
> *holiness adorns your house*
> *for endless days, O LORD.*

► Chapter 1 ◄

# Stable

## Wind and Waves Obey Jesus

I heard a preacher say once that when we give our heart to Jesus, then all of our problems are over. Let me ask you a question. When the storms come up in your life what seems to happen to your faith? Is it replaced with fear and condemnation? Do you feel that maybe you have done something wrong? Not every problem that comes our way is because we are doing something wrong.

*Matthew 8:23-26 NKJV*

*23 Now when He got into a boat, His disciples followed Him.*

*24 And suddenly a great tempest arose on the sea, so that the boat was covered with the waves. But He was asleep.*

*25 Then His disciples came to Him and awoke Him, saying, "Lord, save us! We are perishing!"*

*26 But He said to them, "Why are you fearful, O you of little faith?" Then He arose and rebuked the winds and the sea, and there was a great calm.*

*Mark 4:40 NKJV*

*40 But He said to them, "Why are you so fearful? How is it that you have no faith?*

*Matthew 8:27 NKJV*

*27 So the men marveled, saying, "Who can this be, that even the winds and the sea obey Him?"*

When Jesus got into the boat, the Bible says that the disciples followed Him. Friends, we need to follow Him into the boat, but just because we do doesn't mean that there isn't going to be any stormy weather.

We will have many occasions to face problems in our lifetime. God is still the one who controls the seas. I would rather face any storm with God then to face one without Him. So, if that means we need to get into the boat then, by all means, let's get into the boat!

*Matthew 8:24 NKJV*

*And suddenly a great tempest arose on the sea, so that the boat was covered with the waves. But He was asleep.*

This is not a suddenly that we like to talk about. If we could, we would just as soon avoid it altogether. What did we do wrong here? All we did was get into the boat with Him.

Now all of the sudden, it feels like the world is coming to an end and all Jesus is doing is sleeping! It looks like He doesn't even care that we are perishing. Jesus was not concerned about the wind or the waves because He already knew where He was going. He already knew the storm was not going to stop Him. In fact, it was not affecting Him at all. He continued to sleep until the disciples woke Him up in their desperation.

I believe that He was trying to get the disciples to see something that could have been overlooked by them. I don't want to be dogmatic and say that He was rebuking them for their fear and lack of faith. It is possible that He might have been expressing to them how to respond or react in a positive way, with confidence towards the approaching danger. Jesus gives us a vivid, living illustration, of how to correct this kind of dilemma in our lives. We should be able to speak a God-breathed, God-inspired, Word that packs a wallop!

*Mark 4:39 AMP*
*And He arose and rebuked the wind and said to the sea, Hush now! Be still (muzzled)! And the wind ceased (sank to rest as if exhausted by its beating) and there was [immediately] a great calm (a perfect peacefulness).*

7

*Mark 4:41 AMP*
*And they were filled with great awe and feared exceedingly and said one to another, who then is this, that even wind and sea obey Him?*

As I study this Scripture, one line seems to just jump off the page to me, *"Who can this be?"* Obviously, it is quite apparent that the Word spoken here is in reference to Jesus. What keeps echoing in my ears is the Word, *"Who can this be?"* Could this be you? Could it be possible, that He wants' to see you speaking to the wind and the waves just as He did?

When fear and doubt come, they bring along with them every sort of condemnation; the devil will try to keep you feeling like a failure so that you won't respond with the faith that has been given to you be God.

Remember the story told about Job's friends? When they were sent to encourage him, they only spoke words that cut him to the heart. Accusations were repeatedly spoken to him trying to get him to curse God and then die. The way out of his situation came by Job praising God and not by cursing Him.

Do you have some of Job's friends that live in your neighborhood? Can you hear them saying, *"Well, if you had not been doing this or that, if you had only just obeyed God in the first place, you would not have suffered all this loss?"*

The disciples had not done anything wrong. Up to this point they had only gotten into the boat with Jesus. They were following the Master of the wind. The Master was teaching them how to overcome stormy weather. We can face the storm knowing that God is with us everywhere we go. Now listen, there are Christians who are doing all sorts of things that they should not be doing and they are receiving horrific complications in their lives because of it. God has made a way of escape for them too. It starts with a word, repentance. Today, our country is trying to do away with the term. Repentance simply means to *"turn away from, or to change your mind and go in another direction."*

Doctrines of demons have been placed in some of our churches. One good doctrine, tolerance, has been perverted. They say, *"Its okay son, God forgives you for all that sin in which you are habitually living."* The truth is that God will forgive you, but there is a price to pay. Sin will take you further than you want to go, and cost you more than you want to pay, but when you call out to God you can be sure that the answer is on the way. Forgiveness is just a repentant prayer away.

*1 John 1:9-10 NKJV*
*9 If we confess our sins, He is faithful and just to forgive us our sins and to cleanse us from all*

*unrighteousness.*

*10 If we say that we have not sinned, we make Him a liar, and His word is not in us.*

When you have been cleansed by the forgiving power of God there is nothing like it! This huge weight falls off your shoulders and you feel like you can hold your head up once again. God's forgiveness will restore all of your confidence. Then when God gives you something to do you are not under a heavy load of burden and condemnation.

As a prison chaplain I meet people every day whose past conduct gives them little confidence in their own prayer life. They want me to pray for them because they are looking for results or answers and they feel unworthy to receive by their own prayers. Once they repent from all of the things that have kept them in bondage they become tremendous prayer warriors. All of my confidence is in the working power of God's Word. My confidence rests only in His saving grace and all that He has provided for me. He paid the price of my sin in full for me at the cross. He paid the price in full for you also.

*Matthew 8:25 NKJV*
*25 Then His disciples came to Him and awoke Him, saying, "Lord, save us! We are perishing!"*

10

When the waves were covering the ship the disciples cried out, *"Lord, save us!"* God can see very well what is happening in our lives, and if we will call out to Him, He will bring us our desired peace. With every wave that rises up against you, there is a stronger force that God is just waiting to activate through your faith for you.

We need to get some things stable in our lives. We need to learn how to bring these raging storms in our lives to a standstill. Have you ever seen the person that changes with everything that comes their way? One minute they are up, and then the next minute they are down.

To be stable means to be firm, steady, not likely to break down or fall apart: firm in character and purpose; not likely to change.

We become more stable when we are standing in our blood-bought position in Jesus Christ. God is saying to them and to us, *"Just stand, stand there, and keep your character."*

*Ephesians 6:13 NKJV*
*13 Therefore take up the whole armor of God, that you may be able to withstand in the evil day, and having done all, to stand.*

We need to learn how to plant our feet firmly in Christ Jesus, making Him our strong foundation.

11

When you are standing in the ocean and the waves are crashing down on you, if you try to face the waves head-on, they will knock you down and roll you across the bottom of the ocean floor like a rag doll. But if you take your stance, still in the waves, but standing sideways to them, you have stability in your stance. You can then rock from one leg to the other without losing your balance. Learn to take your stance in Christ with each foot planted firmly in His Word.

> *Ephesians 6:14-18 NKJV*
> *14 Stand therefore, having girded your waist with truth, having put on the breastplate of righteousness,*
> *15 and having shod your feet with the preparation of the gospel of peace;*
> *16 above all, taking the shield of faith with which you will be able to quench all the fiery darts of the wicked one.*
> *17 And take the helmet of salvation, and the sword of the Spirit, which is the word of God;*
> *18 praying always with all prayer and supplication in the Spirit, being watchful to this end with all perseverance and supplication for all the saints—*

When the seas of trouble come your way, stand firm and don't break down. No matter what the circumstances, no matter what they look like, stand there and say, *"Lord, I'm Yours and I don't care what the world is saying to me. I'm standing fast in what You've given me. Thank You for helping me to face this giant in my life.*

*I will forever praise Your Name. You, O God, are worthy of all praise, for You are the One Who rules the raging seas; when its waves rise, You still them."*

God will help you rebuke the wind and the sea. Let me ask you one more question. Who could this be that even the winds and the waves listen to Him? Could this be YOU? Is He speaking to even you?

## Driven and Tossed by the Wind

*James 1:2-8 NKJV*

*2 My brethren, count it all joy when you fall into various trials,*

*3 knowing that the testing of your faith produces patience.*

*4 But let patience have its perfect work, that you may be perfect and complete, lacking nothing.*

*5 If any of you lacks wisdom, let him ask of God, who gives to all liberally and without reproach, and it will be given to him.*

*6 But let him ask in faith, with no doubting, for he who doubts is like a wave of the sea driven and tossed by the wind.*

*7 For let not that man suppose that he will receive anything from the Lord;*

*8 he is a double-minded man, unstable in all his ways.*

## JENNIFER: A PERSONAL TESTIMONY

When our daughter Jennifer was eighteen months old, she was lying on the floor in the living room one night. I went to pick her up and she began to scream in pain. Her little legs had started swelling and just to touch her brought excruciating pain. By the time we got her to the hospital in Osage Beach, Missouri, both legs had swollen up as big as my arms. The doctors in the emergency room took many tests to determine what was causing the problem.

It wasn't until the next morning that we received word about her condition. They couldn't understand just how it could have happened, but it appeared that she had been bitten by an insect found in the country of Indonesia. They said that it was a deadly bite with no known antidote. The swelling would travel up her body until it reached her lungs where she would then suffocate and die. We had just had a missionary from Indonesia at our church earlier that week. We guessed that the insect could have been brought over to our country in his luggage.

When I walked into the room early that morning,

my wife was frantically pacing back and forth across the room like a caged animal. I watched her as she tried to figure out just what we were going to do. We had already lost one child before his first birthday and the thought of losing another was almost more than we could bear. After hearing the bad report I was just standing there, speechless. My wife screamed at me saying, *"For God's sake, Wayne, why don't you do something?"* I didn't have time to think about what I was going to do, but these Words from God came up out of my spirit. *"I guess I will do something whenever you are through."*

We both knew at that moment that God was speaking a Word into our hearts. The waves of death were crashing down upon us and we needed to hear a Word that would bring peace to this out-of-control situation that was staring us in the face. The silence that followed my outburst was broken with God's powerful Words from His Bible; just as if He had us on His mind when He wrote it. I opened my Bible and began to read out loud from the book of James. At that time, I was only a baby in Christ and I didn't even know where to look for the answers I so desperately needed. I just opened my Bible to James and began reading.

There are two different words used in the Greek for our word *"word"*. One is the *Logos* word which is the written Word or Scripture. The second one is *Rhema* which is a God-breathed, God-inspired, Word spoken to us now.

15

*James 1:2* says, *"My brethren, count it all joy when you fall into various trials,"* Count it all joy, for what? How could I count it all joy that my baby was dying? No, God was telling me that I could count it all joy because He is my deliverer and my healer. He is at the helm of my ship, steering me into a safe haven. We both knew that this was a rhema Word from God, spoken at the right moment.

The more I read the Word over my baby, the more I could feel faith begin to rise up in my heart. My faith was being tested and was producing patience. Wisdom was coming to me liberally and without reproach, just like the Word said it would.

*James 1:5-8 NKJV*
*5 If any of you lacks wisdom, let him ask of God, who gives to all liberally and without reproach, and it will be given to him.*

*6 But let him ask in faith, with no doubting, for he who doubts is like a wave of the sea driven and tossed by the wind.*

*7 For let not that man suppose that he will receive anything from the Lord;*

*8 he is a double-minded man, unstable in all his ways.*

As I read His Word out loud where my wife and I both could hear it, we were receiving a gift from God called faith. We were planting our feet in His Word for stability and our focus was no longer on death being the outcome. Now we believed for life and that much more abundantly, above all that we could ask or even think!

*Romans 10:17 NKJV*
*17 So then faith comes by hearing, and hearing by the word of God.*

James writes that we need to activate our faith by doing what the Word says to do:

*James 1:22 NKJV*
*22 But be doers of the word, and not hearers only, deceiving yourselves.*

It also says in *Mark 16* that believers shall lay their hands on the sick and they shall recover. It does not mean just preachers, evangelists and prophets. No, it says believers! That means that I am qualified to pray for the sick. I was a believer so I activated my faith and laid hands on Jennifer and spoke God's Word over her.

*Mark 16:17-18 NKJV*
*17 And these signs will follow those who believe: In My name they will cast out demons; they will speak with new tongues;*

17

*18 they will take up serpents; and if they drink anything deadly, it will by no means hurt them; they will lay hands on the sick, and they will recover."*

It also says in His Word that we should watch and pray. I really wished that I had left my eyes open, because when I opened my eyes after praying, the swelling had gone down completely in both legs. All that remained as evidence showing there had been anything wrong were little bruises where some small blood vessels had broken due to the swelling.

*1 Peter 2:24b* says, *"…by His stripes you where healed."*

We confessed His Word over her and she was healed. I called the doctor and told him that I wanted to take my daughter home. They had not been giving her medication up to this point. He started to argue with me until I told him that I did not have any insurance. There was no argument that the swelling had definitely gone down. He allowed us to take her home if we promised to bring her back if the swelling returned.

They said that they could do nothing for her, there was no cure, yet they wanted me to bring her back in. I felt that what they wanted to do was just help her die as painlessly as possible.

We did take her back to the doctors two weeks later for a checkup. The doctor could not understand how she could be okay. My five-year-old daughter, De'An, told this educated doctor that Jesus had healed her!

*Matthew 21:16 NKJV*
*16 and said to Him, "Do You hear what these are saying?"*
*And Jesus said to them, "Yes. Have you never read, 'Out of the mouth of babes and nursing infants You have perfected praise'?"*

*1 Corinthians 1:27 NKJV*
*But God has chosen the foolish things of the world to put to shame the wise, and God has chosen the weak things of the world to put to shame the things which are mighty;*

The doctor was so impressed that he did not charge us for any of the visits! The hospital itself was a different story, but we had to learn to trust God in that raging sea also. Our response to this real life storm was vital to the outcome of it. Had we not acted on the Word, I am convinced that we would have lost our baby.

## Planting Our Feet Firmly

*James 1:5-8 NKJV*
*5 If any of you lacks wisdom, let him ask of God, who gives to all liberally and without reproach,*

*and it will be given to him.*

*6 But let him ask in faith, with no doubting, for he who doubts is like a wave of the sea driven and tossed by the wind.*

*7 For let not that man suppose that he will receive anything from the Lord;*

*8 he is a double-minded man, unstable in all his ways.*

Applying the Word of God to our situation is planting our feet firmly into the only one who can give us stability. Let's take a look at another familiar portion of Scripture.

*Psalm 107:23-26 NKJV*

*23 Those who go down to the sea in ships,*
*Who do business on great waters,*

*24 They see the works of the LORD,*
*And His wonders in the deep.*

*25 For He commands and raises the stormy wind,*
*Which lifts up the waves of the sea.*

*26 They mount up to the heavens,*
*They go down again to the depths;*
*Their soul melts because of trouble.*

God said that He is the one who raises up the stormy

wind.

We say, *"Oh, God, the devil is coming against me!"* God is saying, *"I'm just turning up the heat a little, son."* With every wave that comes, it's going to clean something off that doesn't need to be in your life.

*"But God, that's the devil."*

*"No, don't you call Me the devil!"* Now God doesn't bring sickness and disease upon us. Come on, we all should know better than that, but there are some sufferings and trials that come to the body. Nobody likes to hear about suffering. Now, we are not talking about suffering with sickness; we do not have to put up with that. There are trials that come our way, testing that comes our way, and tribulations that come our way, and that is what He says in the book of James.

> *James 1:12-14 NKJV*
> *12 Blessed is the man who endures temptation; for when he has been approved, he will receive the crown of life which the Lord has promised to those who love Him.*
> *13 Let no one say when he is tempted, "I am tempted by God"; for God cannot be tempted by evil, nor does He Himself tempt anyone.*
> *14 But each one is tempted when he is drawn away by his own desires and enticed.*

So when the testing comes, it is because we are lusting after something that we want more than Him. That's when we start seeing trouble. God will turn up the heat.

Do you know how you can tell when gold has been refined to perfection? It is when you can look and see your image or reflection on the surface after all of the dross, which is made up of waste products or impurities that float on the surface of molten metal during smelting, has been removed. God is looking to see His image, not just on the surface, but all the way down to your center core. When the heat gets turned up and the dross comes up to the top, it doesn't feel too good. Have you ever had dross come up to the top? *"Oh, yeah, I've had big pieces come up!"* There are problems that come our way that are sent from the devil. We need to learn to discern the difference between God sending us to where we will be tried, and the trials themselves that come from the devil.

> *Psalm 107:26-27 NKJV*
> *26 They mount up to the heavens,*
> *They go down again to the depths;*
> *Their soul melts because of trouble.*
> *27 They reel to and fro, and stagger like a drunken man, And are at their wits' end.*

What is He waiting on? He is waiting for you to call out on the Lord. As Christians, he has given us all power and authority in the Earth in His Name; yet without Him, we can do nothing. He is just waiting on you to call out to Him.

> *Psalm 107:28-29 NKJV*
> *28 Then they cry out to the LORD in their trouble, And He brings them out of their distresses.*
> *29 He calms the storm, So that its waves are still.*

Are there some storms coming against you, against your church, against your pastor? Is everybody asking, "*What is going on?*" Don't worry because God is speaking to these storms, saying, "*Stormy weather, be still.*" He is guiding you to that perfect place of peace and safety.

> *Psalm 107:31-32 NKJV*
> *31 Oh, that men would give thanks to the LORD for His goodness, And for His wonderful works to the children of men!*
> *32 Let them exalt Him also in the assembly of the people, and praise Him in the company of the elders.*

Call on the Name of the Lord and give praises to His Name. Give Him thanks in the middle of a raging storm. He will make you stable!

► Chapter 2 ◄

# Endurance

## Caught Up in a Storm

*Acts 27:9-10 NKJV*
*9 Now when much time had been spent, and*
*sailing was now dangerous because the Fast was*
*already over, Paul advised them,*

*10 saying, "Men, I perceive that this voyage*
*will end with disaster and much loss, not only of*
*the cargo and ship, but also our lives."*

God had revealed something to Paul here and he
started praying. The prayers that Paul prayed were cried
out in intercession and they changed the course of the
lives of the other men on that ship. Paul had a divine
destination and a divine purpose for his life. He knew
where he was going because the Lord had spoken to
him earlier. I also believe he was very concerned about
the other men on the ship. Praying for others is one
way to put God's love into action.

*Acts 27:11-14 NKJV*
*11 Nevertheless the centurion was more*
*persuaded by the helmsman and the owner of the*

*ship than by the things spoken by Paul.*

*12 And because the harbor was not suitable to winter in, the majority advised to set sail from there also, if by any means they could reach Phoenix, a harbor of Crete opening toward the southwest and northwest, and winter there.*

*13 When the south wind blew softly, supposing that they had obtained their desire, putting out to sea, they sailed close by Crete.*

*14 But not long after, a tempestuous head wind arose, called Euroclydon.*

Another way to say *"But not long after"* could be that a *"suddenly"* came upon them. A tempestuous head wind arose. The Amplified Bible describes it as *"a violent wind [of the character of a typhoon]"* I was in a typhoon once while serving in the United States Navy in the mid-1970's. We were in it for only three days, and that was three days too long!

They were warned by Paul what would happen, yet they would not listen. Church, God also has been sending warnings over and over again, and we keep hiding our heads in the sand and ignoring them. Now we are being tossed around by every wave and are even tempted to give up on hope of ever being saved. We put ourselves into an enormous amount of danger by choosing to follow our own wisdom rather than God's.

*Acts 27:15-21 NKJV*

*15 So when the ship was caught, and could not head into the wind, we let her drive.*

*16 And running under the shelter of an island called Clauda, we secured the skiff with difficulty.*

*17 When they had taken it on board, they used cables to undergird the ship; and fearing lest they should run aground on the Syrtis Sands, they struck sail and so were driven.*

*18 And because we were exceedingly tempest-tossed, the next day they lightened the ship.*

*19 On the third day we threw the ship's tackle overboard with our own hands.*

*20 Now when neither sun nor stars appeared for many days, and no small tempest beat on us, all hope that we would be saved was finally given up.*

*21 But after long abstinence from food, then Paul stood in the midst of them and said, "Men, you should have listened to me, and not have sailed from Crete and incurred this disaster and loss.*

I always hated to hear those famous words, *"I told you so!"* Well, now we are in desperate need of help. We have tried it our way so now it's time to do it His way.

*Acts 27:22-25 NKJV*

*22 And now I urge you to take heart, for there will be no loss of life among you, but only of the ship.*

*23 For there stood by me this night an angel of*

*the God to whom I belong and whom I serve,*

*24 saying, 'Do not be afraid, Paul; you must be brought before Caesar; and indeed God has granted you all those who sail with you.'*

*25 Therefore take heart, men, for I believe God that it will be just as it was told me.*

## A Promise from God

Paul gave the men on the ship a word and a promise from God. This was a promise that was given to him because he prayed through to the answer. We need more people like Paul that will intercede for the lives of men and women around the world. We need to come out from hiding in the closet and speak out about what God is saying to people today. This is where you will begin to see the persecution and the suffering come into play. The devil will try to shut you up. Don't you let him shut you up, ever!

*Acts 27:30-31 NKJV*
*30 And as the sailors were seeking to escape from the ship, when they had let down the skiff into the sea, under pretense of putting out anchors from the prow,*

*31 Paul said to the centurion and the soldiers, "Unless these men stay in the ship, you cannot be saved."*

We cannot escape from the drama that is lying before us by abandoning ship. Take your stand in Christ Jesus and ride over the waves that are trying to beat you down. You have to stay in the boat in order to be saved, meaning rescued. I have seen people that have tried to walk away from the things of God saying, *"I just don't want any more of this."* What has happened next in their lives is that they have become miserable.

We need God's stability and the endurance about which Paul is talking here. Do you know how many days they went through that storm? Fourteen days went by before they saw the manifestation of the answer from God. It will take a lot of endurance to get through a major storm in your life; you have to make up your mind that you will never quit until you win.

## A Float Trip: A Gift from My Wife

My wife purchased a deep sea fishing trip for me one year. Over one hundred people from our church were planning to go on this trip. It was early in the year and the weather conditions were unstable, but we went anyway. That morning when we pulled away from the docks we were hit with over four-foot swells while still in the harbor. By the time we cleared the harbor and headed out to the open seas, we were being hit by over twenty-foot swells. When we returned from this trip, I teasingly asked my wife if she had increased my life insurance policy because maybe she knew something that I didn't.

We were scheduled to be out to sea for twelve hours, but it seemed like weeks. We were bound and determined to fish no matter what the weather conditions were. The waves began tossing us around like our boat was a toy. One of the men crossed the upper deck trying to get to some cover. The boat was lifted up in a swell and he squatted down, trying not to lose his balance. Next, the boat dropped out from under him; leaving him in midair! When the boat began to rise again it met him in the air and once again he was standing on the deck. He had landed on the edge of the ship. If he would have come down a little further to his right we would have lost him to the sea!

For safety, most of us moved into the galley, which is a ship's kitchen. Over two-thirds of the people were getting seasick, including more than half the crew. We didn't have any business being out there on the sea in those weather conditions. The storm continued for twelve hours. Can you just imagine what it would have been like to be out there, with Paul, for fourteen days? There were people lying all over the deck moaning and there was a terrible smell coming from everyone that was getting sick. Even if you didn't have a problem with seasickness, being around all of that horrible smell was enough to make you sick.

I spent three years in the navy and never once got seasick, but the conditions were right on that fishing trip for one of those first-time experiences! The company with whom we had chartered this deep-sea fishing trip should not have put our lives in danger like that. I figured that they didn't want to return our money so instead they took chances with our lives. Since this was a church outing we were well equipped to pray our way through the stormy weather. We began giving thanks to the Lord for our safe return to the shore. In order to be delivered from the clutches of the threatening storm, we could not afford to get caught up in complaining.

God lives in the praises of His people and we needed His presence on the boat in the worst way. God, who is rich in mercy and grace, led us back to a safe haven with no loss of any life. When we returned to port we found out that a hurricane had been reported in the area and had spawned several tornadoes that had hit the coast.

There are many people that are going through storms in their homes, business, and churches. You are being tossed around and feel hopeless. There is a voice from God that is speaking to you today that can bring you to the place of peace and hope that you need. God will comfort your hearts. God will never leave you nor forsake you. Speak the Word of God over your storm and let God calm the waves for you. He is right there, right now, by your side.

You know what's really funny? They wouldn't listen to Paul before the storm, but now, all of a sudden, they were all ears. Paul got to a place while praying where he heard the voice of God. Remember, that's where faith comes from. And the voice that he heard lined up with God's Word and Paul started speaking by faith what he had heard God say, *"DON'T BE AFRAID."*

I can imagine their responses. *"What do you mean, 'don't be afraid?"* They were concerned then just like you might be right now. *"Man, we've been in this storm for fourteen days and we have thrown everything overboard that we can think of. We are to the point where we have nothing left."* It's going to take endurance to beat a storm. The definition for endurance is: the act, quality, or power of withstanding hardship or stress, or the state or fact of persevering; continuing, survival.

## Enduring Hardship

*Acts 27:33-36 NKJV*

*33 And as day was about to dawn, Paul implored them all to take food, saying, "Today is the fourteenth day you have waited and continued without food, and eaten nothing.*

*34 Therefore I urge you to take nourishment, for this is for your survival, since not a hair will fall from the head of any of you."*

*35 And when he had said these things, he took bread and gave thanks to God in the presence of them all; and when he had broken it he began to eat.*

*36 Then they were all encouraged, and also took food themselves.*

Up to this point they had been under constant pressure and in need of an answer from God. Now, Paul encouraged them to take something to eat and prepare for God's promises to come to pass. They broke bread together and gave thanks to God. This is a major key to success in coming through any storm.

We need to learn how to praise God while we are still in the problem. You may need to remind yourself of how many times God brought you through former storms. Your rewards are within your grasp, so you must not quit now!

*Hebrews 10:32 NKJV*
*32 But recall the former days in which, after you were illuminated, you endured a great struggle with sufferings:*

Do you remember how David had told the king that he was able to defeat the lion and the bear? Now, he was going to do the same thing with this uncircumcised (indicating Goliath did not bear the mark of having a covenant with God) Philistine. We can find this in *1 Samuel 17:36*. Like David, encourage yourself by remembering those times in your past where God has brought you through a major storm. It will help bring to you a confidence to endure and receive the promises. God is faithful and He is always right on time.

*Hebrews 10:35-36 NKJV*
*35 Therefore do not cast away your confidence, which has great reward.*

33

*36 For you have need of endurance, so that after you have done the will of God, you may receive the promise:*

The disciples were out in the boat in *Mark 6:45-52* and the seas were working against them. They were rowing with great difficulty, trying to get to their destination. This passage states that they where straining at rowing.

*Mark 6:47-48 NKJV*
*47 Now when evening came, the boat was in the middle of the sea; and He was alone on the land.*
*48 Then He saw them straining at rowing, for the wind was against them. Now about the fourth watch of the night He came to them, walking on the sea, and would have passed them by.*

Then Jesus comes up to the boat. It even says that He would have passed them by. Had they not called out to Him, they probably would have been rowing until morning!

*Mark 6:49-50 NKJV*
*49 And when they saw Him walking on the sea, they supposed it was a ghost, and cried out;*
*50 for they all saw Him and were troubled. But immediately He talked with them and said to them, "Be of good cheer! It is I; do not be afraid."*
Think about this. You are caught up in some major

storm in your life. You are getting exhausted from all the work that you have done trying to get through the mess. Here is where you need Jesus to intervene in your life. It is not time for you to give up. The enemy is just trying to throw a smokescreen up in front of your face. Call out to Jesus and He will be there to bring you over into a safe harbor. Don't let Jesus just pass by your boat without your calling out to Him! He is the only one that can rescue you. I have watched men in prison who have gotten really close to getting paroled, and just before they were to be released something came and upset them. Sometimes, this caused them to react in an improper way and then boom! They got into trouble and messed up what was right within their grasp. We need to keep our focus and stop looking at the problems. It could cost us the victory.

*Matthew 14:26-32 NKJV*
*26 And when the disciples saw Him walking on the sea, they were troubled, saying, "It is a ghost!" And they cried out for fear.*
*27 But immediately Jesus spoke to them, saying, "Be of good cheer! It is I; do not be afraid."*
*28 And Peter answered Him and said, "Lord, if it is You, command me to come to You on the water."*
*29 So He said, "Come." And when Peter had come down out of the boat, he walked on the water to go to Jesus.*
*30 But when he saw that the wind was*

*boisterous, he was afraid; and beginning to sink he cried out, saying, "Lord, save me!"*

*31 And immediately Jesus stretched out His hand and caught him, and said to him, "O you of little faith, why did you doubt?"*

*32 And when they got into the boat, the wind ceased.*

Have you ever been caught in a riptide? I experienced one during a ministry trip to Honduras. I had already struggled for a long time in the riptide's powerful current, trying to escape and get back to shore. Almost at the place of exhaustion a member of our ministry team saw my predicament. He stood with his feet firmly planted on the ocean bottom and reached for me. I grabbed hold of his hand and he pulled me in where I could get my feet planted on the bottom also. I had endured and now was safe.

*Acts 27:35-36 NKJV*

*35 And when he had said these things, he took bread and gave thanks to God in the presence of them all; and when he had broken it he began to eat.*

*36 Then they were all encouraged, and also took food themselves.*

In the storm on the ship Paul gave thanks and ate. The Lord is inviting you to commune with him, to break bread together with Him. Oh, that man would praise the Lord for the wonderful works that he has done for them. When you feel like saying, *"What's the use in trying anymore"* or *"I'm getting nowhere fast. I might as well give up."* This one thing you need to know; you are very close to your prize. You are at the place where God steps in and your miracle comes. We were holding a service at the state maximum security prison in McAlester, Oklahoma. It was one of those great services where you felt like you could just reach out and touch God. There were many of those men that were in desperate places in their lives.

Laughter began to break out all over the auditorium. One of the inmates laughed so hard that he fell out of his chair and onto the floor. One of his friends came over to me after the meeting and thanked me for the service. He said that his friend was in a really low place and he needed to laugh like that. I saw the man standing next to the door. So I went over to talk to him. He asked me if I had a Word from God for him. I replied that I couldn't give him a Word from God unless God gave me one. I won't make one up.

However, while I was saying this to him the Lord did give me a Word for him! I told him that he would be getting out sooner than he thought. *"What does that mean?"* He asked.

*"Well, when do you think that you will be getting out?"*

*"In six months,"* he answered back. *"Well,"* I replied, *"you will be getting out before that date."*

Right before you get what God has promised you, it seems like it gets really tough. I asked him how bad his situation was and he said that it was really bad! I told him that that meant that he was really close. He got out three months before his scheduled date to be released! Hallelujah!

Keep your focus on the Lord. Don't look at the wind and the waves. Don't be caught just talking about your problems, speak to the mountain and it shall be moved. Hold on to the promise of God, for you have been enabled with the ability to endure!

## ► Chapter 3 ◄

# Ability
# God's Enabling Power

## Not my Way, but Your Way

Now, we've got to learn how to stop doing things in our own ability, and start doing them in God's ability. Then we can begin to sense the victory even in the heat of the battle. We are not capable of standing with any kind of stability in a storm or to even endure the intensity of the situation without being positioned in Christ Jesus. There is a position in which we need to learn to see ourselves standing, with Jesus. How you see yourself can change the outcome of any situation. It is not a position in which you can place yourself. It is one into which Jesus sets you, but it is still your choice whether or not to go with it. Glory to God for His grace!

*1 Timothy 1:12-14 NKJV*
*12 And I thank Christ Jesus our Lord who has enabled me, because He counted me faithful, putting me into the ministry,*

*13 although I was formerly a blasphemer, a persecutor, and an insolent man; but I obtained mercy because I did it ignorantly in unbelief.*

*14 And the grace of our Lord was exceedingly abundant, with faith and love which are in Christ Jesus.*

This word enabled has something that we need to look at that will help us visualize our positioning better.

ENA'BLED: To give legal power. Supplied with sufficient power, physical, moral or legal. Let's take a look at the same Scripture out of the Amplified Bible.

*1 Timothy 1:12-14 AMP*

*12 I give thanks to Him Who has granted me [the needed] strength and made me able [for this], Christ Jesus our Lord, because He has judged and counted me faithful and trustworthy, appointing me to [this stewardship of] the ministry.*

*13 Though I formerly blasphemed and persecuted and was shamefully and outrageously and aggressively insulting [to Him], nevertheless, I obtained mercy because I had acted out of ignorance in unbelief.*

*14 And the grace (unmerited favor and blessing) of our Lord [actually] flowed out superabundantly and beyond measure for me, accompanied by faith and love that are [to be realized] in Christ Jesus.*

Say this with me, "*Thank you God that you have enabled me (granted me the needed strength and made me able) and have counted me faithful."*

Okay, God has enabled me. So what does that mean? He's not only going to give you the power you need, but also the authority that must go along with it. He is the source of power, strength, wisdom and ability to do what you need done to help you in your hour of crisis.

The meaning of Grace: the simplest way to define such a complicated word is this: God's unmerited favor. We do not deserve it nor could we ever earn it. Out of the love of the Father He made available forgiveness when what we really deserved was His judgment. It also means that we have God's enabling power! As mentioned before, He has given us legal power. God has given us a legal right to speak to the storm. There is another word with the same meaning of "enable" which is ability. Ability is active power, or power to perform; as opposed to capacity, or power to receive.

*1 Timothy 1:14 AMP*
*14 And the grace (unmerited favor and blessing) of our Lord [actually] flowed out superabundantly and beyond measure for me, accompanied by faith and love that are [to be realized] in Christ Jesus.*

We need to get this picture of His grace (unmerited favor and blessing) overflowing to such a great degree that it is superabundantly going beyond the usual.

Well, if God's grace is His unmerited favor, then we need to look at the word *favor* for a moment. How do you find favor with God? I have had men ask me to pray for them just before they were scheduled to go before the judge. They asked me to pray that they would have favor with him. I answered them by saying that as long as we can pray scripturally I would pray.

> *Proverbs 3:3-4 AMP*
> *3 Let not mercy and kindness [shutting out all hatred and selfishness] and truth [shutting out all deliberate hypocrisy or falsehood] forsake you; bind them about your neck, write them upon the tablet of your heart.*
> *4 So shall you find favor, good understanding, and high esteem in the sight [or judgment] of God and man.*

Walking in mercy towards others and walking in truth is the way to find favor with God and man. That is what the Old Testament says to us, so let's look at what the New Testament tells us.

> *Colossians 3:8-10 AMP*
> *8 But now you yourselves are to put off all these: anger, wrath, malice, blasphemy, filthy language out of your mouth.*
> *9 Do not lie to one another, since you have put off the old man with his deeds,*
> *10 and have put on the new man who is renewed in knowledge according to the image of*

*Him who created him,*

Are you walking in kindness and mercy? Are you walking in truth? If you are not, then you cannot expect to find favor with God, let alone man, or in the case of the inmate who was seeking favor, from God, through the judge. Jesus is our example here on this Earth. He came as a man to show us how we can overcome stormy weather in this life by the power of the Holy Spirit and the revelation of the word spoken through the power of the Holy Spirit.

> *Luke 2:52 NKJV*
> *52 And Jesus increased in wisdom and stature, and in favor with God and men.*

There is an increase that can come in the favor that you have with God. Make the choice to walk in God's ways and then watch what happens.

> *Psalm 30:4-5 NKJV*
> *4 Sing praise to the LORD, you saints of His,*
> *And give thanks at the remembrance of His holy name.*
> *5 For His anger is but for a moment,*
> *His favor is for life;*
> *Weeping may endure for a night, But joy comes in the morning.*

Wow, His favor lasts for a lifetime. This is good news for you and me. I like walking in God's favor. We travel all over the world and have seen the favor of God firsthand. When you are walking in His favor you will find that He makes things happen for you for your good. We have prayed for customs agents in other countries to receive Jesus as their Lord and Savior and we now have great favor when going through customs! I have pictures of four customs agents lying on the floor weeping from the personal way that God reached out and touched them with His power while we prayed for them.

We went into Honduras right after hurricane Mitch struck in 1998. Although we had just returned from a trip there, a man gave us over $500,000 worth of vaccination medication for the victims of the storm. The man that gave it to us explained that he gave it to us because he would not send it without an escort. Things have a way of disappearing, and he wasn't taking any chances.

We met a doctor traveling with another ministry team that was a brother of a friend of mine. I told him that I had papers that would help them get their medicine into the country without any problems. We had favor with the head of customs because we had led him to the Lord on an earlier trip. We had a bus waiting and with only five of us coming down this time we had plenty of room to take the other group anywhere they wanted to go. He was excited about the prospect of receiving such help and told his team leader, but the reply from this leader surprised me when he responded

44

that they didn't need our help.

The doctor told him that maybe he should reconsider, but he insisted that he didn't need our help. They already "had things arranged, so thanks, but no thanks." When we arrived at the airport, we were greeted by the head of customs, which is our friend. "Amigos!" He cried out so loud you could hear him clear across the airport. He slung his automatic weapon up on his shoulder and started picking up our stuff, escorting us swiftly through the airport to our bus that was waiting out front.

Right before leaving customs, I asked the leader of the other group if he was sure that he didn't need our help. He was still being indifferent for some reason so we went ahead and left. When we got back to Tulsa, we found out that this same group leader spent about nine hours trying to get out of customs because of the medicine his team was bringing with them. The bus that was to pick them up got tired of waiting and left. The bus driver had to go and pick up someone else. This group leader that "didn't need our help" went and told everybody that I had abandoned him at the airport!

If you walk in mercy and truth, then you will have favor with God and man. He could have had the same favor that we had, as God is no respecter of persons. God does not love anyone any more or any less than anybody else. We were simply walking in favor. He also had the same favor, but because he was not willing to humble himself and let us help him he lost the peace and ease with which God could have taken him through customs.

Before leaving for any trip to do a work for the Lord we are always checking ourselves for anything that could hinder the trip. Unforgiveness and resentment will keep you from receiving the benefits of God's favor working on your behalf.

Say this with me:

*"I have favor with God and with man, because I choose to walk in mercy and truth. I like favor, I have favor and favor belongs to me. God has given to me, enabled me, counted me faithful, and put me in the ministry. His grace (unmerited favor, blessing, and ability) overflows in me to such a great degree that it is superabundantly going beyond the usual, Amen!"*

*1 Timothy 1:14 AMP*
*14 And the grace (unmerited favor and blessing) of our Lord [actually] flowed out superabundantly and beyond measure for me, accompanied by faith and love that are [to be realized] in Christ Jesus.*

As the writer here in Timothy goes on to say, this grace is accompanied by two powerful words, *faith* and *love* that are (to be realized) in Christ Jesus. Faith means to have total dependence on God. When Adam sinned he was separated from God and moved into doing things his own way, becoming independent of Him. This attitude can only end up in total defeat. Sooner or later we will realize the mistake of our own ways. Until then, doubt and unbelief will mark us and we may find ourselves staggering with every wave that comes in, knocking our feet right out from under us.

Instead, we depend on God's ability to move us out of our inability and over into the realm of faith, trusting totally on someone far greater than ourselves.

Just one Word from God produces faith. Once we finally see our position, the one in which God has placed us, we can begin to take our stand in Christ Jesus and move out to speak to the storm. First, however, we need to be a part of the body of Christ. You can try to do a lot of things that the Bible says to do, but if you are not one of God's children it will not work for you.

*Ephesians 2:8-10 NKJV*
*8 For by grace you have been saved through faith, and that not of yourselves; it is the gift of God,*
*9 not of works, lest anyone should boast.*
*10 For we are His workmanship, created in Christ Jesus for good works, which God prepared beforehand that we should walk in them.*

From where does faith come?

*Romans 10:17 NKJV*
*17 So then faith comes by hearing, and hearing by the word of God.*

When you know that God has spoken a Word to

you it doesn't matter what the reports of the storms are anymore. You have been moved out of one position over into another. You now need to move out in obedience to the Word that you have heard. Obeying the Word activates the faith which was given to you by God in that Word. You must do something with this Word that you have heard. You must act upon it.

> *James 2:17 NKJV*
> *17 Thus also faith by itself, if it does not have works, is dead.*

God has equipped us with power and the legal authority to perform His Word in the Earth. First, you receive faith from a Word that God spoke to you, then you must activate it, put it into action, or it just becomes a dead word. Have you ever heard the person that is always telling you what he is going to do, but he never does it? You want to tell him to stop talking so big and just do it. You have been given the ability to do it now. Take your stand in Christ, move out of your inabilities and cross over into His ability. Someone might ask you, *"Just who do you think you are, God?"*

*"No sir, but I am one of His representatives on the Earth."* We have been authorized to act as an official delegate or agent for Christ. We have been created in His image and we should reflect His glory in the Earth.

*1 Timothy 1:12*
*12 And I thank Christ Jesus our Lord who has enabled me, because He counted me faithful, putting me into the ministry,*

The Word that Paul received from the angel of the Lord that night, in Acts chapter 27, gave faith to those that heard his report. He spoke truth and comfort to the men on the ship because he spoke words that represented the love of the Father.

The second important word Paul used in *I Timothy 1:14* was love. As it says in the book of 1 John, God is love

*1 John 4:16 NKJV*
*16 And we have known and believed the love that God has for us. God is love, and he who abides in love abides in God, and God in him.*

God does more than just love us, He is love. It is His nature to love us and He gives this nature to us, so that we can live with Him and in Him. God loves those that are believers in His Son with a special love. But God also loves the whole world with that same special love!

*John 3:16-17 NKJV*
*16 For God so loved the world that He gave His only begotten Son, that whoever believes in Him should not perish but have everlasting life.*
*17 For God did not send His Son into the world*

*to condemn the world, but that the world through Him might be saved.*

## LOVE

Two distinct Greek words for love appear in the Bible. The word *phileo* means to have ardent affection and feeling, a type of impulsive love. The other word, *agapao,* means to have esteem or high regard. Let's take a look at the agapé love for a moment.

• *Agapé* love indicates the nature of the love of God toward His beloved Son *(John 17:26),* toward the human race generally *(John 3:16; Rom 5:8),* and toward those who believe on the Lord Jesus Christ *(John 14:21).*

• *Agapé* love conveys God's will to His children about their attitude toward one another. Love for one another was a proof to the world of true discipleship *(John 13:34-35).*

• *Agapé* love also expresses the essential nature of God *(1 John 4:8).* Love can be known only from the actions it prompts, as seen in God's love in the gift of His Son. *(1 John 4:9-10).* Nelson Study Bible

God's love is not the same as our love. It is unconditional. We put conditions on our love. *"You do this and then I will love you."* If we have a good pleasant feeling about someone, then we can love them. The agapé Love of God is not an emotion. If we would learn how to walk in the God kind of love, which is by choice and not by feelings, then we would see more clearly how God looks at us.

50

We do not deserve God's grace (unmerited favor) yet He has given it to us without measure. He enabled us with His power and legal authority to represent Him here on this Earth. He also has given us His Word that produces faith, and when that faith-giving Word is acted on, it brings us victory in our storms. We know this because He loves us, for that is His nature. Once we get a revelation of just how great His love is, it will bring confidence to us to face any storm that crosses our path. All the necessary arrangements have been made for any weather conditions we may encounter. We are in full possession of a stable, enduring ability that can sustain us while going through stormy weather.

## Hero From the Past

Let's take a look at an example of one of our heroes from the past, Moses.

He started out wanting to be a help to some Israelites against their oppressors. In his own attempt at bringing justice, he caused the death of an Egyptian. Later, while trying to settle a dispute between two of his Hebrew brethren they asked him if he was going to kill them too, just like he had done to the Egyptian *(Exodus 2:11-14.)* For fear of being found out by Pharaoh, Moses fled, ended up on what the King James Version calls the backside of the desert, and hid there for a long time. It was a good place for him to go. On the backside of the desert, as a shepherd, he received instructions and experience on

51

how to be a shepherd of God's people. When God told Moses to go and speak to Pharaoh, he had absolutely no confidence in himself. He had to learn how to become stable and firm in character, his purpose not likely to change under the intensity of the assignment or the position in which God would place him.

> *Exodus 3:11-14 NKJV*
> *11 But Moses said to God, "Who am I that I should go to Pharaoh, and that I should bring the children of Israel out of Egypt?"*
> *12 So He said, "I will certainly be with you. And this shall be a sign to you that I have sent you: When you have brought the people out of Egypt, you shall serve God on this mountain."*
> *13 Then Moses said to God, "Indeed, when I come to the children of Israel and say to them, 'The God of your fathers has sent me to you,' and they say to me, 'What is His name?' what shall I say to them?"*
> *14 And God said to Moses, "I AM WHO I AM." And He said, "Thus you shall say to the children of Israel, 'I AM has sent me to you.'"*

Moses was still having trouble with this whole scenario and was looking for a way out.

> *Exodus 4:1 NKJV*
> *1 Then Moses answered and said, "But suppose*

*they will not believe me or listen to my voice; suppose they say, 'The LORD has not appeared to you.'"*

*Exodus 4:13 NKJV*
*13 But he said, "O my Lord, please send by the hand of whomever else You may send."*

When God calls us to do something like this for Him, we will have to come to a place where we empty ourselves of our fleshly desire to do our own thing, and overcome any fears of being inadequate to the task.

Having done this, we then need to have confidence, in God's Word, that we can overcome the storms that are ahead. This is when it is going to require a stable, enduring ability to wait for God's timing. Moses had learned to become stable in God. Endurance is another strong point that he had to learn. It is really easy to give up just before we see the results of that thing for which we have been standing in faith.

When you speak up for God, know this, it will be carried out in His timing and not yours.

*Exodus 5:22-23 NKJV*
*22 So Moses returned to the LORD and said, "Lord, why have You brought trouble on this people? Why is it You have sent me?*

*23 For since I came to Pharaoh to speak in Your name, he has done evil to this people; neither have You delivered Your people at all."*

53

All of the plagues were to be directed at those that were outside of God's house. His people would be protected from the curse, but when you are in the middle of the storm it can seem like it is being directed right at you.

God sent a Word to inform the people that he was working things out for their good. However, due to all the additional pressures being placed on them by the Egyptians, they could not see how God was going to rescue them out of cruel bondage. God's message was sent to encourage them to follow him through a major storm that would soon fall on Egypt.

*Exodus 6:5-9 NKJV*

*5 And I have also heard the groaning of the children of Israel whom the Egyptians keep in bondage, and I have remembered My covenant.*

*6 Therefore say to the children of Israel: 'I am the LORD; I will bring you out from under the burdens of the Egyptians, I will rescue you from their bondage, and I will redeem you with an outstretched arm and with great judgments.*

*7 I will take you as My people, and I will be your God. Then you shall know that I am the LORD your God who brings you out from under the burdens of the Egyptians.*

*8 And I will bring you into the land which I swore to give to Abraham, Isaac, and Jacob; and I will give it to you as a heritage: I am the LORD.'"*

*9 So Moses spoke thus to the children of Israel;*

*but they did not heed Moses, because of anguish of spirit and cruel bondage.*

Here we can begin to see where this stable, enduring ability came into full view. Moses had been placed into a hurricane-sized storm, and it was necessary for him to stand strong in faith. Moses was standing firm in the character that God had molded into him. The enemy had not been able to make him fall apart in the face of opposition. He was standing steady on his course and was not likely to change. He was stable. During forty years on the backside of the desert he had been taught great lessons in endurance, and he needed to remember those lessons to withstand the present storm to its end.

It is going to take an ability, which is the active power to perform that goes beyond man's inability, to finish riding any storm into a safe haven. God has enabled man with not only the power, but also the legal authority to bring it to pass.

Moses was 80 and Aaron was 83 years of age and they had to trust totally in God to do what He said He would do. It was simply not possible to do it in their own abilities. In spectacular displays of power, one after another, every one of the plagues demonstrated God's superiority over all the gods in which Egypt put her trust *(Exodus, Chapters 4 - 11)*. Not one stone would go unturned as God set the stage for releasing Israel from 400 years of bondage. The outcome would prove without a doubt that there is no God like Jehovah!

The keys of stability, endurance and ability were now activated and the rescue mission for overcoming stormy weather was set into motion.

One more step occurred just before God delivered the final death blow that caused Pharaoh to let them go free. God instituted the Passover sacrifice of the Lord.

*Exodus 12:24-28 NKJV*

*24 And you shall observe this thing as an ordinance for you and your sons forever.*

*25 It will come to pass when you come to the land which the LORD will give you, just as He promised, that you shall keep this service.*

*26 And it shall be, when your children say to you, 'What do you mean by this service?'*

*27 that you shall say, 'It is the Passover sacrifice of the LORD, who passed over the houses of the children of Israel in Egypt when He struck the Egyptians and delivered our households.'" So the people bowed their heads and worshiped.*

*28 Then the children of Israel went away and did so; just as the LORD had commanded Moses and Aaron, so they did.*

I see a remarkable similarity between what took place here in Exodus, and what happened with Paul in the storm in *Acts 27:33-38.* Just before each of these storms ended they were each instructed to break bread together and give thanks to God. The children of Israel had the Passover and Paul broke bread with the ship's crew. This brought them encouragement and physical nourishment that would cause them to press forward through their storms.

The blood sacrifice of the Passover is seen as a means of deliverance. It is a feast of hope and life. It represents deliverance and new beginnings. When you find yourself in stormy weather, break bread with the Lord. Have a time of communion with Him. Just the presence of the Lord can bring you peace.

In both of these stories they had to continue in their struggles to reach their desired haven. To give up right then would only bring them disaster. The devil continued to try to kill Paul even after he had witnessed the appearing of the Angel of the Lord. Moses was chased all the way to the Red Sea; where, likewise, it looked like he would not escape.

*Exodus 14:10-12 NIV*
*10 As Pharaoh approached, the Israelites looked up, and there were the Egyptians, marching after them. They were terrified and cried out to the LORD.*

*11 They said to Moses, "Was it because there were no graves in Egypt that you brought us to the desert to die? What have you done to us by bringing us out of Egypt?*

*12 Didn't we say to you in Egypt, 'Leave us alone; let us serve the Egyptians'? It would have been better for us to serve the Egyptians than to die in the desert!"*

Does this sound like something that could have slipped out of your mouth, just before you reached your goal?

> *Exodus14:13-14 NIV*
> *13 Moses answered the people, "Do not be afraid. Stand firm and you will see the deliverance the LORD will bring you today. The Egyptians you see today you will never see again.*
> *14 The LORD will fight for you; you need only to be still."*

Once again we see in this passage God's grace, or enabling ability, as he brings them through the Red Sea. I can also see a type and shadow of the death, burial, and resurrection of Christ in the description of what happened here in *Exodus 14:21-31*, as they entered into the sea and emerged on the other side. Their enemy was swallowed up, never to be seen alive again by Israel.

> *Exodus 15:1-3 NIV*
> *1 Then Moses and the Israelites sang this song to the LORD:*
> *"I will sing to the LORD,*
> *for he is highly exalted.*
> *Both horse and driver*

*he has hurled into the sea.*
*2 "The LORD is my strength and my defense;*
   *he has become my salvation.*
   *He is my God, and I will praise him,*
   *my father's God, and I will exalt him.*
*3 The LORD is a warrior;*
   *the LORD is his name.*

Make a decision today to walk away from your own way of life. Repent and give your life to Jesus before it is too late for you. I don't say this to scare you but to warn you that you don't have that much time left.

Get into the boat with Jesus. This is your only way of escaping the stormy weather that is sure to come. There is tremendous advantage in being in the boat with Jesus. He is with you and will never forsake you.

## CONCLUSION

You can walk into almost any church around the world, and find a storm brewing just under the surface.

The possibility of the storm exploding into a full blown hurricane at any moment should put us all on alert. By looking at the faces of most people, you might think that all is well. The real facts are being concealed under those smiles which look like they are painted on.

The voice of the Father has been preparing us for what is coming. He has equipped us with everything that we need to be victorious in any storm that might come our way. In the days that lie ahead, we will witness the Bible come alive in our modern-day world.

Here is an example which we experienced firsthand. God was reaching out to warn and protect His children from a treacherous storm.

In November, 1998, a tropical depression sat off the coast of Honduras, Central America. For three days it hovered just off the coastline and dumped eighty to ninety inches of rain on the land. It never moved on shore, but what the rain did to the countryside was catastrophic.

Hondurans are very serious about their football. The United States was playing against Honduras one time while we were down there. The USA actually won the game, and for the first time in Honduras, I felt like my life might be in danger, namely, from the football fans! Anyway, while this tropical storm was inundating the country with rain, Honduras was at the end of their football season for that year. The storm had developed into a Category One hurricane called 'Mitch', which was determined, by someone, to not be much of a threat. For this reason, the news media decided to concentrate on the football game instead of the storm!

The rivers began to swell over their banks and the waters were running off of the mountains causing flash floods all across the nation. Roads and bridges were being washed away and travel across the country was almost impossible. No one was alerted about the flooding and people were waking up in the middle of the night with water washing away their homes. There were whole villages that were swept downstream, leaving the remains of what looked like riverbeds. In one village, the only thing left standing was a church building. Had the people been warned, they would have been able to save the lives of many that died that night. The death toll during this storm soared to over 15,000 with some 26,000 still missing.

This tragedy was so unnecessary. Seven years later another hurricane occurred just like this one, but they had learned from their previous mistakes. The people were warned early enough about this second storm so they could take precautions and the death toll was only just a little over one hundred people this time.

As the country was sleeping during the first storm little or no concern was given to the impending danger that loomed just off the coastal shores. It was a common belief from the people across the nation that God had judged them for their wickedness and unrepented sins.

There was no doubt that the nation had received a devastating blow from this terrible storm, but, to add sorrow upon sorrow, we heard statements that this was God's judgment. That idea only brought more confusion and misery. When we sense that there is something getting ready to happen we need to inform the people so that they can have adequate time to respond. What happened there was tragic, because they were not informed in time to respond.

There is nothing wrong with enjoying sports or other things that give us enjoyment out of life. Please don't think

I am saying watching football is sinful. I am not saying that at all. What God is saying to us is to heed His warnings. Get ready to respond to the storms that are coming. It is not God's nature to destroy us like that. The Bible says that Satan is the one who comes to steal, kill, and destroy. When we hear evil reports we need to seriously consider what God's Word has to say on the matter.

*John 10:9-10 NKJV*
*9 I am the door. If anyone enters by Me, he will be saved, and will go in and out and find pasture.*
*10 The thief does not come except to steal, and to kill, and to destroy. I have come that they may have life, and that they may have it more abundantly.*

This storm had settled in and was hovering just off the coastline of Honduras; we were informed that we could not fly into the country until it passed. Every day we watched the weather reports, waiting for the storm to move up the coast so we could catch the first flight to Honduras.

I had a dream one night that we were walking into a village. Everything seemed okay, but suddenly the villagers turned on us and began shooting at us. As we were running away someone said *"There is safety in the city!"* I then woke up and I was thinking that that was not a good dream to have right before I went on a mission's trip. With each day that passed by, the thought that we might not see some of our friends again was weighing heavily on my mind. We had already purchased our tickets to go on this mission's trip to Honduras long before the storm had come on the scene.

When the news came in that the country was devastated, over half of our team decided that they shouldn't go. I figured that God already knew this was going to happen before we had even purchased the tickets, so He must have a plan to use us in Honduras. For this reason, we went out on the first scheduled commercial flight. God gave me a Scripture:

*Psalm 20:1-2 NKJV*
*1 May the LORD answer you in the day of trouble; May the name of the God of Jacob defend you;*
*2 May He send you help from the sanctuary, And strengthen you out of Zion;*

I had no idea what that meant at the time, but I was soon going to find out.

When we were finally given the go-ahead to fly into Honduras, the news of what this storm had done was overwhelming. The major airlines would only fly into the capital city Tegucigalpa, and then we would have to take the local airline Taca into San Pedro Sula, which is the second largest city in the nation, and our destination. The water level had been over six feet deep at the airport in San Pedro Sula. For fear of the runway collapsing under the weight of the larger planes, they prohibited them from landing there.

Over one-third of Tegucigalpa was washed away. Thirty-foot waves went down the streets carrying away all that was in their path. When people found out we were going to Honduras, they began to send us all kinds of medicine, food, and clothing to take down there with us.

One doctor gave us equipment such as surgical lamps, hospital beds, wheel chairs, and much more so that we could set up two mobile clinics. We had more than two forty-foot containers full of supplies. Both Dole and Chiquita Banana Companies lost all of their crops, which would take years to grow back. Since they didn't have produce to transport, they used their ships to bring aid to devastated Honduras. The Hondurans said that it would take at least eleven years just to recover the country to its pre-storm conditions.

It was then that I understood the reason behind the Scripture that God had given me from *Psalm 20* regarding sending help from the sanctuary. There were many people opening up their hands and hearts to help in the recovery effort. The government officials had made a decision to turn over the task of distribution of medicine and food to the church. They reasoned that the church had a closer relationship with the people and could make better assessments of the damages and needs in their local districts.

At this time the reports of lives lost was over 15,000 and rising. There were some 26,000 people still missing.

Many of the communities had been cut off from outside assistance and communications were gone. For this reason they could not get accurate casualty reports. Major roads and bridges were ruined, making it impossible to get to everybody who needed help. The death toll kept climbing and I wondered where it would all end. We had met with the head of the Honduran Homeland Security. We have since become good friends and visit with him when we are in the country. He was working with the Honduran president trying to bring sanity back to the nation. He was instrumental in getting us in touch with the Vice President of Honduras.

He also helped us to get our containers full of life-saving supplies off the docks and through customs! God was showing us His favor because not many other containers were released. We were working with the Pastor's Association and it took less than one hour to empty both containers and send the much-needed relief to its destinations. Before the storm, a group of pastors in San Pedro Sula had been praying because they sensed something was getting ready to happen. Their prayers had a significant part in the outcome, because very little damage was done to the city.

One of the pastors Misael Argeñal, pastor of the largest Foursquare Gospel church in Central America, felt that the churches needed to circle the city for seven days. On the seventh day after going around the city seven times, pastor Misael flew over the city in a helicopter and anointed it with oil. Many of the people thought that he was crazy, because all seemed safe and secure, with no sign of impending danger in sight. However, Pastor Misael was faithful to obey the instructions that he received from God. When we were approaching San Pedro Sula, we saw total devastation all around the city. People were living in huts that they had made out of debris. Up and down the major highway for miles you could see the huts amidst the devastation and loss.

When we reached the city limits, in stark contrast, it was like nothing had ever happened! The city was completely untouched by the storm. Someone referred to this city as the lungs of Honduras. *"This is where you could feel the breath of God,"* they said. San Pedro Sula became a major source of help and a refuge for the nation. Thank God that these pastors obeyed the voice of God. We found that out of all of the people that had lost their lives only two percent were on a church roll. Factories were closed down everywhere, except one factory that was owned by a Christian. His factory was still open for business because none of his employees had died. The people were saying that God was judging their nation; but God was saying, *"He who dwells in the secret place of the most high shall abide under the shadow of the Almighty." (Psalm 91:1)*

He was protecting His sheep, He was protecting His children. In the story where Paul was traveling to Rome in Acts, chapter 27, he had tried to warn the people of the coming danger. They did not heed the warning and it cost them dearly. Praise God that Paul was praying for the lives of those that were sailing with him. Praise God that someone had the courage to go against what other people were saying and follow God's directions. We can learn from the mistakes of others and not follow in their footsteps. Take the message of the Gospel and strengthen yourself in Christ Jesus. Become a stable individual that God can use to help people overcome the stormy weather of life. Endure hardship like a good soldier. Move out of your inabilities into God's ability and change the outcome of the storm. Learn to speak out His Word with boldness. God will enable you to complete your assignment. Don't be afraid to move ahead.

*Psalm 107:8 NKJV*
*8 Oh that men would praise the LORD for his goodness, and for his wonderful works to the children of men!*

On another mission's trip to Honduras, in November of 2007, I had a chance to visit with my friend from the Honduran Homeland Security. He said that he had been visiting with the President and they agreed that the economy of the nation was devastated after 'Mitch' in 1998. There seemed to be no way that their economy could sustain their financial needs after that hurricane. However, after only two short years they discovered that their country was back on its feet and progress was being made much faster than the projected eleven year recover period!

They said that if it were not for all of the Christian efforts being poured into Honduras from countries around the world they would have still been in a slump and unable to recover.

Don't let the storms in your life destroy you. Listen to the words of advice that people of God are speaking to you. Don't receive a lie from the devil and think that the storm just off the coast has no effect on you. It's only a tropical depression anyway, right?

The devil has deceived mankind into believing that good is bad and bad is good. Satanic churches are being established all over. The religion of Wicca is gaining a legal access into our public places of worship. Major storms are heading this way, friends, and you need to ask yourself just whose side you are on. God has only good things planned for you.

*James 1:17 NKJV*
*17 Every good gift and every perfect gift is from above, and comes down from the Father of lights...*

Satan has only destruction planned for you, and killing is his nature. He will rob you of all your joy and point his finger at God demanding an explanation as to why all this can be happening to you; as if God is the one who is responsible for it. We serve a just God, and righteousness and goodness make up His character. There is a penalty for unrighteousness that must be paid. His allowing us to freely break His laws would make Him an unjust judge. Adam forfeited his position to rule the Earth because he broke God's law.

Satan would love to see God forfeit his position of reigning as King by God breaking His own laws. Jesus took a beating for us to satisfy the requirements of God's law. He was crucified on a cross and buried. He was in hell for three days where he snatched away the keys of hell, death, and the grave. Jesus defeated Satan once and for all at his own game.

Friends: justice has been served. The penalty has been paid in full. Jesus has triumphed over the unjust death sentence that your adversary had planned for you. You must make a decision on which side you choose to be. Let me put it to you this way: as long as you refuse to make a decision, then you have, in fact, already made one.

*Matthew 5:25-26 NKJV*
*25 Agree with your adversary quickly, while you are on the way with him, lest your adversary deliver you to the judge, the judge hand you over to the officer, and you be thrown into prison.*
*26 Assuredly, I say to you, you will by no means get out of there till you have paid the last penny.*

It was hard for me to understand why I would have to agree with the adversary, Satan, in this Scripture. Really, I thought there was nothing that we could even remotely agree on, except I hated him and he hated me, and on that we could agree. If I don't agree with him about my sin, and repent, then God has no choice but to allow justice to run its course. By not repenting I would end up in jail paying for something for which Jesus has already paid in full.

The devil would even let you blame him for all of your problems, thus keeping you from the truth. As long as you don't own up to it if you have sinned, and keep blaming it on someone else, the devil has a right to you and can enforce a verdict of guilty on the charges brought against you.

In *Matthew 12:30* Jesus says, *"He who is not with Me is against Me..."* It is your decision. Now is the time to choose, but remember, there are consequences to the choices that you make in life.

> *1 John 1:8-10 NKJV*
> *8 If we say that we have no sin, we deceive ourselves, and the truth is not in us.*
> *9 If we confess our sins, He is faithful and just to forgive us our sins and to cleanse us from all unrighteousness.*
> *10 If we say that we have not sinned, we make Him a liar, and His word is not in us.*

God has made a way to escape the storms that are sent to destroy you. I would rather be in the boat with Jesus when the wind and waves begin to rise than apart from His presence in any circumstance.

*Acts 3:19 NKJV*

*19 Repent therefore and be converted, that your sins may be blotted out, so that times of refreshing may come from the presence of the Lord,*

Let us move forward with the confidence and boldness that come only with knowing who we are in Christ Jesus. This is the stability that packs a strong defense against the enemy's plan of attack against you. As you become stable in God's Word you can drive out the forces of every storm that would challenge you. With endurance and ability that goes beyond your own, you can strike fear in your enemy that will send him on the run!

You have been given a legal right to speak to the storms that confront you, with the authority of the King of Kings and Lord of Lords is backing you up. I can see Jesus standing at the helm of the ship, speaking to the wind and the waves, saying, "Peace be still," with all those around Him asking, "Who can this be?"

I tell you in great honesty and great truth from the Word of the Lord, this can be you!

God wants you to receive His free gift of salvation. Jesus wants to save you and fill you with His Holy Spirit more than anything. If you have never invited Jesus, the Prince of Peace, to be your Lord and Savior, I invite you to do so now. Sincerely pray the following prayer and you will experience a new life in Christ Jesus.

# Prayer for Salvation

*Lord God, You loved the world so much, You gave Your only begotten son to die for my sins so that whoever believes in Him will not perish, but have eternal life. The Bible says that we are saved by grace through faith, as a gift from You. There is nothing I can do to earn salvation. I believe and confess with my mouth that Jesus Christ is Your Son, the Savior of the world. I believe He died on the cross for me and bore all of my sins, paying the price for them. I believe in my heart that You raised Jesus from the dead. I ask You to forgive me of my sins. I confess Jesus as my Lord. According to the Bible, I am saved and will spend eternity with you! Thank You, Father. I am so grateful!*

*In Jesus Name,*
*Amen.*

*John 3:16 NKJV*
*16 For God so loved the world that He gave His only begotten Son, that whoever believes in Him should not perish but have everlasting life.*

**Notes:**

## About the Author

Rev. Wayne Sanders is a graduate of Rhema Bible Training Center. Along with his wife Connie Sanders, they co-founded "Common Ground Ministries."

They serve as Chaplains in seven prisons. Wayne is also an accomplished psalmist and a ministers in street evangelism. He teaches and preaches the Word of God in churches all across the United States and on the foreign mission field.

For those people who will not come to church Common Ground Ministries takes the Church to them.

# ORDER PAGE

To order additional copies of: How to Overcome Stormy Weather, complete the information below:

Ship To: (please print)

Name_____

Address_____

City:_____ State: _____Zip:_____

How to Overcome Stormy Weather

Suggested donation: $10.95

I would like to order ___copies of the book. $_____

Postage and handling $3.14 per book $_____

TOTAL AMOUNT $ _____

For your charitable contributions
Make Checks Payable To:

Wayne W. Sanders, or Common Ground Ministries

Visit our website where you can order through our
PayPal account: www.cgmok.com

Mail To: Common Ground Ministries
PO Box 2811
Broken Arrow, Oklahoma 74013

- **FREEDOM**
**The Liberty that Repentance Brings**
*An Investigation of True Repentance*

*by Jerry W. Hollenbeck*
- **The KINGDOM of GOD**
**An Agrarian Society**
*Featuring The Kingdom Realities, Bible Study Course,*
*Research and Development Classes*

- **The Word of God**
**FATHER • WORD • SPIRIT**
**Literally THE WORD**

----

*by Mary Ann England*
- **Women in Ministry**
*From her Teachings at the FCF Bible School - Tulsa, Oklahoma*
*Compiled and Edited by Charles R. England*
*(Foreword by Pat Harrison)*

----

*by James Jonsten*
- **WHO is GOD to YOU?**
The path to know the most misunderstood name in the universe.

----

*by Aaron Jones*
- **In the SECRET PLACE of THE MOST HIGH**
*God's Word for Supernatural Healing, Deliverance and Protection*

- **SOUND from HEAVEN**
*Praying in Tongues for a Victorious Life*

**Available at Select Bookstores and**
**www.BOLDTRUTHPUBLISHING.com**